An Introduction to CLASSICAL EDUCATION

❧

A Guide for Parents

Christopher A. Perrin, MDiv, PhD

www.ClassicalAcademicPress.com

For more information on Dr. Perrin's speaking and consulting, see page 46.

An Introduction to Classical Education:
A Guide for Parents

© Classical Academic Press®, 2004
Version 2.6

Classical Academic Press
515 S. 32nd St.
Camp Hill, PA 17011

www.ClassicalAcademicPress.com

ISBN: 978-1-60051-020-5

Diagram on page 32 created by Nathan Gerard

Book design by:
Rob Baddorf
Cover design by:
Lenora Riley

As the former headmaster of a classical school, I have often spoken with parents who are both interested in and puzzled about classical education. "How does the classical approach differ from what is offered in public schools?" "Are there any other schools doing what you are doing?" "How do classically educated students perform on standardized tests?" After several decades, the questions are predictable, but wholly justified. Unfortunately for me, even my answers are now predictable, which is one reason I am writing this guide. If you will read this before you talk to me (or someone like me), you can spare both of us my stock replies. Secondly, if I put my answers down in writing, I am bound to say something new.

If you are like most, you have probably heard about classical education by means of a friend who either has a child enrolled in a classical school, or who is homeschooling classically. You are doing your research, and are interested enough to do some reading about classical education. If you have visited a classical school or co-op, you may have seen a few classes in operation which have raised eyebrows, interest, and many more questions. In any case, you have questions—and a good many of you will have put those questions down in writing.

I wish to commend you for your questions, for your thinking. To come up with hard-boiled questions is something that, as you shall see, is quite classical. Classical education is a long tradition of asking questions and digging up answers, consulting others, then asking, seeking, and finding once more. It is joining, as one writer puts it, the "Great Conversation." That means reading great books (the *classics*), studying them, mining them, and talking to others about the influential ideas they contain. Whatever else classical education is, it is an ongoing series of questions and answers. So you see why I am glad you come asking about all manner of things besides the yearly tuition.

Modern Confusion, Ancient Clarity

It is a tumultuous time to be living. Institutions, information, customs, mores, and standards are changing rapidly. Choices and options have multiplied; our culture is becoming increasingly kaleidoscopic. Such colorful and rapid change does have its dramatic element and some find it quite entertaining. However, constant change and novelty can themselves grow old, becoming what Thomas Oden calls "the cheap promise of radical newness" which is "the most boring and repetitious of all modern ideas."[1] Many of us are ready to leave the party, go home, and have a cup of tea in a quiet chair. As we contemplate raising and educating our children, many of us have been forced to ask ourselves what we wish to pass on to our children. How do we nurture them in the midst of all the confusion, doubt, and conflict of this modern world? Is there any place of rest and refuge—any place of tranquility and strength?

Education is that vast undertaking of passing on the wisdom and knowledge of one generation to another. It involves discovery, but also instruction; it is cultural transmission. With our present culture undergoing so much flux, it is no surprise to find that education is in a state of tumult too. For the parent looking for a school to aid in this task of cultural transmission, it is often a bewildering affair.

Those of us in classical education are taking our cues from a time before the party began. Our experiences are all similar: we have not found the wholesome food we need in the present; we have been entertained but not fed, amused but not instructed.

We have gone, therefore, to another place, not too far off, but still forgotten by most. We have gone back to the well-walked

---

1. Thomas Oden, *After Modernity . . . What? An Agenda for Theology* (Grand Rapids, MI: Zondervan, 1990), 21.

path of the tried and proven—the classical method of education. It has never really disappeared; it just became quite fragmented and diffused, with parts like ruins in modern schools and colleges. It was eclipsed as the reigning model only about a hundred years ago after reigning for over a thousand. Your grandparents are likely to have received something of a classical education.

G.K. Chesterton said that every revolution is a restoration—the recapturing and reintroduction of something that once guided and inspired people in the past. The word *revolution* is from the Latin word *re-volvere*—"to re-roll" or "to re-turn." A revolution is that thing which, going around, comes around—again. In a similar vein, C.S. Lewis says that when we have lost our way, the quickest way forward is usually to go home. So we are returning, we are revolving. To put it strongly, we are revolting, and we are doing it by going home.

A Brief History of Classical Education
Sketch and Overview

I hope you will find it refreshing to discover that the method of classical education is simple yet profound, like so many great ideas from the wheel to the umbrella. Its basic philosophy is to teach children in the ways they naturally want to be taught, despite not always knowing it. Put another way, classical educators teach children what they want to know when they want to know it. When children are astonished with the human tongue, we teach them language and grammar. When children are ready to challenge every assumption, we teach them logic. When students are yearning to express themselves with passion, we teach them rhetoric. To be sure, children did not discover this means of education on their own; rather it appears that it was parents who discovered it, and the children merely ratified it.

The phrases *classical* and *classical education* beg for some definition. In history, the *classical period* refers to the civilizations of the Greeks and the Romans (ca. 600 BC to AD 476), who have bequeathed to us classical myths, art and architecture, and the classical languages of Greek and Latin. Certainly the education practiced by the Greeks and Romans can be called *classical* education. *Classical education*, therefore, can mean the educational methods of the Greeks and Romans. However, the word *classical* or *classic* cannot be restricted to the classical period, per se. We also use the term to describe things that are authoritative, traditional, and enduring. Classic literature, for example, can be any work (not just Greek or Roman literature) of enduring excellence. Therefore, we can use the phrase *classical education* to refer not just to the educational practices of the Greeks and Romans, but also to authoritative, traditional, enduring, and excellent education. I use the phrase with both of these connotations in mind: *Classical education is the authoritative, traditional, and enduring form of education, begun by the Greeks and Romans, developed through history, and now being renewed and recovered in the twenty-first century.*

With this general definition in mind, we can now sketch an outline of the history of classical education. After this initial brief sketch, we will come back and paint in some additional detail.

Classical education is old, which is why it now appears so new. It was new with the Greeks and Romans over 2,000 years ago; they are credited with constructing the rudiments of the classical approach to education. We would be misled to think that the Greeks and the Romans educated in simple and consistent ways, for there is a good deal of variety in the curriculum and approach of both the Greeks and the Romans. After all, nearly 1,000 years encompass the period of these two civilizations! Still, there are common themes that run through the educational practices of both groups, including a generally sustained emphasis on the study of grammar, literature, logic, and rhetoric. It was later, during the Middle Ages (ca. AD 500–1460), that the great variety of subjects and approaches present in the Greeks and Romans was analyzed and put into a systematic and more consistent form and curriculum. The curriculum of the trivium (meaning "three ways"), featuring the subjects of grammar, logic, and rhetoric, was formally established during this time, as well as its counterpart, the quadrivium ("the four ways"), containing the subjects of astronomy, arithmetic, music, and geometry. The words *trivium* and *quadrivium* were coined in the Middle Ages, *not* during the period of the Greeks and Romans. I find it helpful to refer to one form of classical education as *trivium-based education*, the kind of classical education being recovered in many K–12 schools and homeschools in North America.

It is important to emphasize that classical education has *evolved*. It has evolved with some sustained themes and patterns, but not without significant variation. The Middle Ages cannot be reduced to a simple educational cliché—it too was varied, despite its penchant for classification and order. In the late Middle Ages, learning began to ebb (the so-called *dark ages*), setting up the need for the Renaissance (ca. AD 1350–1600), which was among other things a cry to return to the learning of the past—to go *ad fontes*, back to the fountain. The Reformation (ca. AD 1517–1700) was a complex movement of spiritual reawakening, but it also contained this element of returning to the ancient fountains of wisdom, with the special emphasis of returning to the authority and teaching of Scripture. The reformers retained the interest in studying classical languages and literature revived by the Renaissance; the great reformers were themselves learned, classically educated men.

The next major movement was the Enlightenment (ca. AD 1700–1789), which marked a departure from the authority of Scripture and the church to an allegiance instead to the power of man's native intellect. Science with its varied subjects came into its own, and while most scientists were also Christians or theists, there was an increasing tendency to study and understand the world without reference to biblical teaching or authority. Still, however, most forms of education retained the rudiments of the trivium and quadrivium. Our founding fathers, for example, were all reared in the Enlightenment period, but bear the marks of classical training in literature, classical languages (especially Latin), history, and rhetoric.

It really is not until the modern period, beginning in the early 1800s, that we begin to see the first signs of the erosion of classical education, but even then we note that this erosion was a slow, gradual process, and throughout the 1800s classical education was still the dominant approach in the United States and Europe. Through the early 1900s, however, this erosion quickened and by 1950 the educational landscape of the United States had clearly shifted from a classical to a "progressive" model. It is this progressive form of education that we have all received, making our knowledge and awareness of classical education limited. It is our progressive educations that make us think of the classical approach as foreign and novel—even though the classical model has reigned for centuries and the progressive model is the novelty.

So there has been variation and change, and in the 1900s notable atrophy. The subjects of grammar, logic, and rhetoric do continue as themes throughout the history of classical education, even though they have ebbed and flowed and been taught in different ways and sequences. Classical methods of education have also continued, which we will consider later in this text. Even after the ascendancy of progressive education, the fragments of classical education persist, even in progressive schools. The scattered stones of classical education are present in contemporary schools and can still be seen by a trained eye. Recovering classical education is a matter of gathering those stones and repairing the ruins.

Painting in the Sketch

Now that we have sketched the outline of classical education, let's retrace this outline and paint in some important details. The Greeks did come first. Precisely because they did come first, they are immortalized as important founders of Western culture and civilization. How it is that they emerged as a potent culture and civilization is its own mysterious and fascinating story, which we cannot explore here. The Greeks have given to us the first enduring forms of democracy (embodied in the Greek city-state or *polis*) and great treasuries of art and literature. Their educational system did evolve and change, but it consistently emphasized the importance of *arête*, or individual excellence and achievement. Physical excellence and ability was just as important (if not more) than intellectual excellence. Greek children from age seven to fourteen attended both a *palaestra*, where they learned to wrestle, and a "music school," where they learned reading, recitation, writing, and arithmetic as well as how to play the lyre and to sing. ("Music" to the Greeks had a much wider meaning than "music" as it is used today.) From age ten to fourteen, students would continue with their physical training at a *gymnasium*, where they studied wrestling, boxing, running, the long jump, and throwing the discus and javelin. These skills had an obvious connection to military training and soldiery. From age fifteen to eighteen, some privileged male students would continue their education by observing and participating in Greek cultural and civic life, being trained and mentored by adult Greek citizens. Finally, some young men from age eighteen to twenty would undergo two years of military training that would prepare them to serve as capable military officers and soldiers.

This general sequence and very basic curriculum was enhanced and changed as the Greek civilization grew. Important Greek educators (sophists and philosophers) emerged who argued for various ways of educating Greek youth. Some advocated training for political success and viewed man as the measure or standard of all things (Protagoras); some advocated a dedicated study of rhetoric that would enable practical political success not just for personal ambition but for the good of the Greek city-state (Isocrates). Still others like Plato (following his mentor Socrates) argued for the dedicated study of philosophy (instead of rhetoric) which he believed would lead men to discover truth, goodness, and justice. Most of these educators valued the study of dialectic (or logic) which enabled students to learn how to reason correctly and detect and refute false reasoning. Aristotle (who succeeded Plato) argued for the study of both dialectic and rhetoric. Ultimately the Greeks passed down their concept of *paideia,* their view that man is to be crafted like a work of art by a standard of excellence (*arête*). As such, education is the making of a man, not the training of a man to do things (vocational training). This conception persists today in our idea of the "well-rounded, liberally educated man."

The Romans conquered the Greeks (in 143 BC) yet found themselves conquered culturally by their Greek captives. The Romans greatly admired and emulated Greek art, architecture, literature, and education. While the Romans did have some of their own educational emphases (such as a commitment to agricultural and military training), they imported the educational subjects, goals, and methods of the Greeks. Thus, while the subjects of grammar, logic, and rhetoric got their start with the Greeks, they continued to thrive under the Romans. Like the Greeks, the Romans started formal education at the age of seven. Students began their studies with a *litterator,* who taught them "letters" or how to read. After learning how to read (in Greek, Latin, or both), the students moved up to a *grammaticus,* who in a school setting taught them not just grammar (the structure, form, and syntax) of language but also literature, particularly poetry. Through the study of literature students also learned history, ethics, and politics; they also did a number of writing exercises that prepared them for rhetoric. Greek students studied Homer (*The Iliad* and *The Odyssey*), who was the model for excellent language, virtue, and wisdom. The Romans eventually studied the Latin writer Vergil (*The Aeneid*), who was the Latin equivalent of Homer. Sometimes students did not study with a dialectic teacher per se, and some students did not study dialectic (or logic) at all. Often the *grammaticus* would teach students some rhetoric near the end of their secondary study, and usually this would end a student's formal course of study. Dialectic (logic) emerged as a field of study from the Greeks, who thought it complemented a student's rhetorical abilities. If a student wished to pursue a political or legal career, he would certainly go on for training in rhetoric, since rhetoric aimed to train students to speak eloquently and persuasively—skills needed both in the assembly and in the courts.

The trivium subjects of grammar, logic, and rhetoric did persist through both the Greek and Roman periods, but in various sequences and patterns. These three subjects were very useful for increasing skill in the use of language, and so are often called *verbal arts*. With the advent of the Middle Ages, four *quantitative arts* were ratified and added to the curriculum: geometry, astronomy, music, and arithmetic. Geometry included some rudiments of geography, astronomy included some physics, grammar included literature, and rhetoric included history. These four quantitative arts were known as the *quadrivium* ("the four ways"), and the seven arts together became known as the *artes liberales*, or the seven liberal arts. A "liberal arts" college, one might think, would emphasize these seven subjects (don't be so sure). These liberal arts were thought to be the arts (or skills) of the free man or the arts which would provide "freedom" to those who studied them. After the formalization of these seven liberal arts in the Middle Ages, a new sequence (though with some variety!) of study evolved. The first three arts (the trivium) were studied first (though rhetoric was often studied later and long) and generally followed by the quadrivium. I hope the diagram on the next page is helpful:

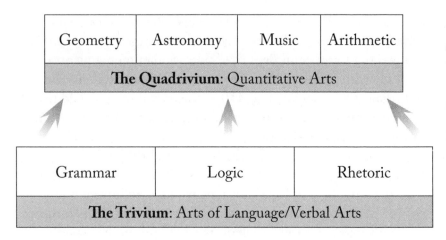

Geometry	Astronomy	Music	Arithmetic
The Quadrivium: Quantitative Arts			

Grammar	Logic	Rhetoric
The Trivium: Arts of Language/Verbal Arts		

Greek and Roman elements of education, therefore, were collected, categorized, and formalized during the Middle Ages. Put another way, the classical educational model inherited from the Greeks and the Romans was modified and updated. It was during this time that the terminology of the trivium and quadrivium was coined, as well as the *artes liberales*.[2] Almost universally, Christians adopted the classical model and invested it with theological assumptions and guidelines that were intended to serve the church. The study of theology was added to the seven liberal arts as the crowning discipline or "queen of the sciences." Christians even continued to study the non-Christian classical authors of the past with reverence and respect, using authors like Aristotle to help create systems of Christian theology (e.g., Thomas Aquinas). It was also during the Middle Ages that a more straightforward and discrete sequence of subjects evolved. Thus it is from the *medieval* trivium (inherited and modified from the Romans) that we derive much of our structure, inspiration, and guidance in our present efforts at recovery (and why I like the phrase *trivium-based education*). It was during the Middle Ages that we witness

---

2. It was the early medieval writer Martianus Capella who gave us the canon of the seven liberal arts (composing the trivium and quadrivium) in his book *The Marriage of Mercury and Philology*. Capella lived from approximately 410–449, but his book peaked in influence in the ninth and tenth centuries.

the rise of the university, where the quadrivium subjects really came into their own in an institutional atmosphere, and where law and medicine first became courses of study. The trivium subjects, especially grammar, continued to be taught by private teachers (tutors) and in cathedral schools and monasteries. Logic and rhetoric were often taught at the university level along with the quadrivium subjects. Cathedral schools were church schools that were attached to cathedrals where students were often sent to receive their education, usually for a fee. Monastic schools offered education to boys who committed themselves to become monks, but also to the poor of a community as the monastery was able. Many of the great minds of the Middle Ages were monks who were educated in monasteries (Dominic, Albert Magnus, Thomas Aquinas).

As we saw in our initial sketch, classical education continued to develop through the Renaissance and Reformation. Both movements represented a return to the learning of the past, particularly the study of the Greek and Roman authors in their original languages of Greek and Latin. During these periods scholars searched for and found many ancient manuscripts of Greek and Roman authors. The study of Greek was revived (very pertinent to the study of the New Testament) after having abated during the Middle Ages. Latin study, which had never ceased, increased. Not surprisingly, in their enthusiasm for these ancient authors, many writers began to imitate the masters they had rediscovered.

Reformers like Martin Luther and John Calvin started schools that emphasized classical subjects and learning. Luther, for example, doubted the value of certain pagan authors like Aristotle (especially his works on ethics) but still urged students to study Aristotle's books on rhetoric and poetics. While stating his preference for school curriculum, Luther says this about the study of classical languages in 1520: "In addition ... there are of course the Latin, Greek and Hebrew languages, as well as the mathematical disciplines and history."[3] Luther assumes as a matter of course that students will be studying not only Latin and Greek, but also Hebrew (the original language of the Old Testament). The reformers emphasized the importance of creating a literate, educated church that could read and study the Scriptures—in the original languages. As inheritors of the classical tradition of education, they took it for granted that students should study an ample amount of history and literature—even of the pagan variety. We see as well the commitment to the quantitative arts (Luther mentioned mathematics) that compose the liberally educated man or woman.

As we touch once more upon the Enlightenment period, it will be sufficient to note that while the religious motive and orientation of education did begin to shift to a naturalistic viewpoint, it is still true that (1) a Christian orientation and motive still continued and in some places increased, and (2) the classical subjects and methodology continued and were adopted by non-Christian theorists and educators. During the Enlightenment, for example, universities came into their own and began to flourish and multiply throughout Europe and then North America. The curricula of these universities were clearly "classical" and linked to the classical tradition which they inherited. Experiment, change, and modification to the classical tradition did begin (especially with the advent of scientific experimentation), but it was in no way abandoned.

Up until the early 1900s, various forms of classical education were the norm for the United States and Europe. The curriculum at Harvard, for example, was non-elective (there were no majors), required for all students until 1884. A record of Harvard's curriculum in 1830 reveals it to be nothing but a classical curriculum in clear connection with the trivium and

---

3. Martin Luther, *Three Treatises* (Philadelphia: Fortress Press, 1978), 94.

quadrivium.[4] Great minds and writers up to this time were all educated classically: people like Abraham Lincoln, Oliver Wendell Holmes, and even early twentieth-century writers like William Jennings Bryant and G.K. Chesterton. People in the generation of C.S. Lewis and J.R.R. Tolkien were some of the last to have been educated classically among the British. Certainly the earlier generations of the American Founders were classically educated: their knowledge of classical language, literature, and history is widely acknowledged by historians and played a fundamental part in shaping the American Constitution and political philosophy. A cursory reading of the *Federalist Papers* proves this point; writers like James Madison, John Jay, Alexander Hamilton, and Thomas Jefferson quote Latin phrases; refer to political precedents and lessons from Greek, Roman, and European history; and write with an elegance and style that astonishes us today.

How, therefore, can such a long tradition of education seem so novel today, at the beginning of the twenty-first century? Well, it only takes one generation to stop the transmission of the past. And education is precisely a matter of passing along what was given to us, or as Chesterton put it, "Education is simply the soul

---

4. The late Harvard Latin scholar E.K. Rand sketches the former Harvard curriculum for us: "I would here call the reader's attention to a page of the Harvard Catalogue for 1830–1831. My copy is unbound, but even when bound, this volume of thirty-one small pages would still be portable. It sets forth the course of instruction for Freshmen, Sophomores, Junior Sophisters, and Senior Sophisters. The programme is founded on the literatures of Greece and Rome, and many of the authors are listed. But there are also mathematics through calculus, general history and ancient history, with 'Greek antiquities,' Grotius, *De Veritate Religionis Christianae,* English grammar, rhetoric and composition, with themes, forensics, and oratory, modern languages, logic, philosophy and theology, natural philosophy, including mechanics, chemistry, electricity and magnetism, with 'experimental' lectures—all this by the end of the Junior year. The great feature of the Senior year is that no Classical literature is prescribed; the ancient authors have been transcended for the higher learning—natural philosophy, including astronomy, optics, mineralogy, and the philosophy of natural history, also intellectual and moral philosophy, and theology both natural and revealed. Modern languages are still pursued, themes and forensics are still required. Finally, we note political economy, anatomy, and Rawle 'On the Constitution of the United States.'" E.K. Rand, *Founders of the Middle Ages* (New York: Dover Publications, 1957), 231.

of a society as it passes from one generation to another."[5] The move away from classical education began in the mid-1800s with the thinking of men like Horace Mann (1796–1859), a Massachusetts educator who worked tirelessly for modernized public education, and was consolidated by later thinkers like John Dewey (1859–1952), who advocated a kind of "progressive" education that emphasized "learning by doing" and rejected many traditional methods like memorization and classical language study. Dewey and the progressive educators emphasized the need to train citizens for the growing, industrialized American democracy.

Throughout the 1920s and 1930s, various forms of progressive education began to take shape and gradually supplanted the classical model. It is true that the classical model never completely disappeared, and its remnants remain in many places (e.g., in the name "grammar" school), but by the 1950s these progressive forms of education became dominant. Most of us, therefore, grew up under the teaching of progressive educators who believed they were ushering in a superior method of teaching and preparing students for life in the modern, quickly changing postwar world. A few examples of the progressive approach should ring familiar: classical languages were dropped altogether and relegated to shrinking classics departments in colleges; basic instruction in phonics and decoding was replaced with a "whole language" approach of reading instruction; training in logic and dialectic was replaced with self-expression without fault-finding; writing instruction guided by imitating the masters and frequent practice was replaced with more individualistic, creative approaches and less practice; math instruction steeped in drill, practice, and repetition was replaced with curricula containing less drill and practice and more activities and stories related to the subject; history instruction

---

5. G.K. Chesterton, *What's Wrong with the World* (San Francisco: Ignatius Press, 1987), 112. Chesterton also writes: "Education is a word like 'transmission' or 'inheritance': it is not an object but a method. It means the conveying of certain facts or qualities, to the last baby born." Chesterton, 161.

grounded in and celebrating the Western tradition from which the United States emerged was gradually replaced with a multicultural approach that downplayed European and even American history and presented instead a smattering of world history (your old social studies classes). Furthermore, progressive educators often looked back on the classical model as harsh, cold, and unpleasant for students. As a result, progressive educators strove to be entertaining and fun, and gradually began to expect less of students in terms of work and achievements. Standards of student behavior also began to change, and schools became more permissive and less willing to discipline for misbehavior. Grading, too, became more lenient in an effort to boost student self-esteem.

In the last twenty years this progressive movement[6] has continued to play out, with some new twists. Philosophical relativism (no universal truths or moral standards) now reigns without rival in popular culture and in education. Its close cousin, philosophical skepticism (nothing can be known with certainty), also maintains a strong presence. As a result, we have seen increasing antagonism for any viewpoint that challenges this modern orthodoxy by daring to declare that any one fact or ethic is actually true or normative. Early programs like "Values Clarification" have continued and multiplied, programs which assume and teach moral relativism. The only real sin in many modern schools is to disagree with the notion that everyone

---

6. C.S. Lewis questions the honesty of "progressive" and "neutral" education, pointing out that even the relativists pursue their own values and dogma: "The important point is not the precise nature of their end, but the fact that they have an end at all. They must have or this . . . book is written to no purpose. And this end must have real value in their eyes. To abstain from calling it 'good' and to use, instead, such predicates as 'necessary' or 'progressive' or 'efficient' would be a subterfuge. They could be forced by argument to answer the questions 'necessary for what?,' 'progressing towards what?,' 'effecting what?'; in the last resort they would have to admit that some state of affairs was in their opinion good for its own sake." C.S. Lewis, *The Abolition of Man: How Education Develops Man's Sense of Morality* (New York: Macmillan, 1947), 40.

determines his own "truth" and his own morality.[7] As you can imagine and probably know, Christians and their viewpoints (creation, fall, redemption) are not generally appreciated (unless of course, they keep silent and just follow along). This relativism has given rise to egalitarianism—that doctrine that no one can really be superior to anyone else (which makes sense when there are no universal standards). Egalitarianism in turn has resulted in grade inflation, the lowering of academic standards (so everyone can get an A), and a hesitancy to recognize outstanding achievement. Parental authority, too, has ebbed considerably. In many public schools, parents are not welcome to observe classes under any circumstances.

The effects of modern education will vary somewhat from region to region and school to school. Nonetheless it is still possible to generalize about the widespread effects that are observed around the nation. It is also true that modern educational research and methods sometimes make useful discoveries and contributions. It is true as well that some educators are returning to traditional methods after continued frustration with educational innovation. Direct Instruction, the Core Curriculum of E.D. Hirsch (author of *Cultural Literacy*); the traditional and virtual charter school model of William Bennett; the Paideia Project of Mortimer Adler; various independent learning centers; and the rise of independent phonics programs and even a renewed interest in Latin study are all evidence of a return to traditional models. Some modern educators, therefore, are surprisingly open to classical education, and some are stumbling upon it without really knowing it, recalling these lines of T.S. Eliot:

> We shall not cease from exploration
> And the end of all our exploring

---

7. Chesterton writes, by contrast: "That is the one eternal education; to be sure enough that something is true that you dare to tell it to a child." Chesterton, *What's Wrong with the World*, 167.

Will be to arrive where we started
And know the place for the first time

The modern experiment in education, therefore, is about 100 years old, and flagging. The classical experiment is about 1,000 years old, and reviving.

Classical Education ... Again

Rather than merely citing the illustrious record of classical education, I wish to cite more modern evidence. I wish to cite the students in classical schools and homeschools. Their delight and joy in their learning are usually the first things prospective parents note. The grammar school students sing and clap out history time lines, science facts, Latin vocabulary, Bible verses, and rules of grammar. They do this throughout the day, usually with great verve and delight. They remember this knowledge set to music with alarming accuracy and permanence. Dialectic (or logic) students, you will witness, spend much of their day arguing with their teachers and peers. Perhaps to the surprise of some, they are encouraged to do this by their teachers, who are charged with the formidable task of teaching them not just to argue, but to argue well. Most will observe that these adolescents seem to enjoy the process. Parents often discover, with some frustration, that such students grow increasingly better at pointing out the fallacies committed in dinnertime conversation by everyone present, including Grandpa. Rhetoric (high school) students have already studied a good bit of grammar and logic; what they wish to do is weave these disciplines into attractive speech and writing. Having learned how to win arguments, they now learn how to win people—for rhetoric is the art of *persuasive* speech and writing. You will find these older students writing a good bit in many genres; you will also find them speaking before their peers as a regular course, whether making a political or forensic speech, or presenting a lab report.

Grammar, logic, and rhetoric are central disciplines in classical schools. You might have noticed that these disciplines also receive emphasis at various stages or periods in the school. Grammar is emphasized during the elementary years (our *grammar* school), logic during the junior high years, and rhetoric during the high school years (see the diagrams on the following pages). Therefore, grammar will be taught in some form in all grades (K–12) but receives special emphasis and attention in grades K–6. The same is true of logic and rhetoric. The assumption here is that these subjects are always operating in some form, but that they are suited to be explicitly taught at certain stages in a child's development. As such, each trivium subject is seen as a "paradigm" or master subject that colors and guides the way the other subjects in the curriculum are taught. For example, virtually every subject in the dialectic school will be taught "dialectically"— students will be arguing, debating, and discussing in math, science, history, and theology classes. In the rhetoric school (our high school), students will be writing persuasive essays and giving speeches in several classes outside of their rhetoric class. Dorothy Sayers argued that the trivium subjects are not really subjects at all but a means or method for handling and learning subjects—a kind of master art (a tool) that enables one to study any subject.[8] She compared each trivium art to a tool, like a chisel or plane, that once mastered can be applied to fashion all varieties of wood (subjects). While we are used to thinking of grammar as a subject (and it has been reduced to a mere self-contained subject in modern schools), it has traditionally been viewed as an all-encompassing discipline or "art." The same is true of logic and rhetoric.

This point cannot be emphasized enough. Our teachers of the last generation have divided knowledge into relatively

---

8. See Dorothy Sayers's speech "The Lost Tools of Learning" (1947), available at https://classicalacademicpress.com/product/the-lost-tools-of-learning-cd/.

isolated "subjects" without emphasizing the interconnection of all knowledge. We have learned "subjects" without actually learning how to tackle these subjects—we have not learned how to learn. We might say that we have been set to work hammering, chiseling, planing, and carving without ever being taught how to use the tools. We have picked up what we could as we went along, incidentally. The classical educators started from the other end and emphasized the importance and use of those master tools that could be widely applied. Of course in order to learn the use of these master tools (grammar, logic, and rhetoric), it is necessary to apply them to some piece of wood, to some subject—and so actual subjects must be studied (English, Latin, history, etc.). But note that the chief goal was to master the tools—for in mastering the tools, the subject (any subject) would soon be mastered as well. We encounter a paradox: classical educators favor tool over content and therefore help students to master more content than ever. They have taught their students how to learn.

Emphasis of Trivium Arts: Paradigmatic or "Tool" Approach

GRADES K–6 GRAMMAR STAGE	GRADES 7–9 LOGIC STAGE	GRADES 10–12 RHETORIC STAGE
Grammar: English and Latin	Grammar	Grammar
	Logic	Logic
Logic		Rhetoric
Rhetoric	Rhetoric	

The shaded and enlarged Grammar, Logic, and Rhetoric boxes indicate that these subjects are dominant and central (paradigm subjects) during the stages in which they occur.

Curricular Subjects Taught from a Grammatical, Logical, or Rhetorical Perspective

K–6		7–9		10–12	
Grammar	Math	**Logic**	Math	**Rhetoric**	Math
	Science		Science		Science
	History		History		History
	Literature		Literature		Literature
	Fine Arts		Fine Arts		Fine Arts
	Bible/Theology		Bible/Theology		Bible/Theology

During each stage, the same subjects are taught but are informed by the unique perspectives of either grammar, logic, or rhetoric.

Sayers also recognized that classical educators tended to teach students these tools at certain developmental stages. As the students age and mature, teachers adjust the manner and means by which they teach. Factual information, grammar, vocabulary, and syntax are emphasized in the grammar school years (K–6), frequently by means of singing and chanting as well as by direct instruction, reading, and discussion. Principles and relations are emphasized in all subjects during the middle school years (our dialectic school, 7–9) by means of reasoning, debate, and discussion, fueled by the dedicated study of logic. Effective and persuasive speaking and writing are emphasized during the high school years (10–12) by means of training in theory, imitation of great writing and speech, and frequent practice. Sayers characterized the grammar stage as the "poll-parrot" stage when students love to memorize, sing, and repeat whatever they encounter. She characterized the dialectic stage as the "pert" stage when students challenge authority, ask "how" and "why," and enjoy arguing and debating. She characterized the rhetoric stage as the "poetic" stage when students are more interested in creative thinking and expression.

The Trivium Arts as Stages in a Child's Development

GRAMMAR	LOGIC	RHETORIC
Age: 5–11	Age: 11–14	Age: 14–18
Poll-Parrot Stage ➡	Pert Stage ➡	Poetic Stage
Language: grammar, syntax, structure, vocabulary	Language: reasoning, debate, clarity	Language: eloquence, beauty, persuasion
Philologists	Philosophers	Poets
Basic facts, fundamentals	Principles, relations	Expressive communication, application, synthesis
Method: singing, chanting, repetition	Method: argument, discussion, debate	Method: discussion, speeches, imitation, practice
Writing: clarity, narrative, description	Writing: compare/contrast, praise/blame, argumentative	Writing: persuasive, legal, polemic, poetic, creative

To be clear then, the words *grammar, logic,* and *rhetoric* have a range of meaning. These words can refer to self-contained subjects or they can refer to a method or art ("tools") of learning all subjects. Finally, they can be used to describe three developmental stages through which children progress.

Latin and Greek

Classical schools are also known for teaching classical languages: usually Latin, but sometimes both Latin and Greek. Latin has been taught in classical schools for centuries, even after it ceased to be a popular spoken language. There is good reason for this, for the study of Latin rewards us richly in several ways.

Latin is a fundamental subject in classical schools and homeschools. It is one of the "paradigm disciplines" of the grammar school, through which students learn the rudiments and structure of language—the Latin language, the English language, and through them the structure of all language. Latin is the mother tongue for over 50 percent of all English words, so the study of Latin greatly enhances one's English vocabulary. Often, just one Latin word is responsible for several English words. Take, for example, the Latin word *porto* ("I carry"). From this word are derived *port, portal, porter, porch, airport, import, important, transport, export, report,* and *portable.* In this case, one Latin word helps yield eleven English words—a pretty good investment.

Latin also helps students understand grammar. As they learn Latin grammar, they are learning or reinforcing their knowledge of English grammar. Our own way of labeling and analyzing English grammar evolved from the study of Latin grammar—all those "grammatical" terms, such as *verb, noun, adjective,* and *adverb,* are all Latin words developed to understand Latin grammar! The grammar of the Latin language is logical, straightforward, and highly regular, making it an ideal language to learn grammar that can be applied to many other languages, including, of course, English.

It has been shown repeatedly that the study of Latin quickens and enables one's mastery of English. SAT and GRE (Graduate Record Exam) scores rise. In fact, the students scoring the highest on the verbal section of the GRE are not English students—but classics majors. Anyone who wants to see the hard, statistical facts demonstrating the value of Latin study is encouraged to visit the website of the National Committee for the Study of Latin and Greek (www.promotelatin.org).

Studying a foreign language early (many classical schools start in 3rd grade with a formal course) has always been the classical way, and is proven wise by experience, for students acquire language fast when young. Students typically learn ten new Latin words a week—with far greater ease than their parents. Students at this age are eager to learn language, and many of them profess Latin as their favorite subject.

Finally, we should mention that Latin is also the mother tongue of the so-called "Romance languages": Spanish, Portuguese, French, Italian, and Romanian. They are called the Romance languages because they directly descended from the language of the Romans—which was Latin. If 50 percent of our words in English come from Latin, up to 90 percent of the words in these languages come from Latin. For example, *porta* in Latin means "door"; *puerta* in Spanish means "door." *Amicus* in Latin means "friend"; in Spanish and Portuguese it is *amigo*, in Italian *amico*, in French *ami*, in Romanian *amic*. When a student learns Latin, he is also doing advance work in these languages given birth by Latin.

If Latin is responsible for 50 percent of our English vocabulary, Greek is responsible for an additional 30 percent. Greek is also the basis for much medical and scientific vocabulary, and has the advantage of being the language of the New Testament, making it very valuable for study in Christian schools. Those who study Latin and Greek will achieve the utmost understanding of English vocabulary and grammar, and will also find that Latin and Greek reinforce one another, since they are both inflected languages (nouns and verbs have variable endings) with a very similar structure.

Those who have studied multiple languages know that after one language has been learned the second and third come much faster and easier. After learning how to fly one kind of plane, pilots are quickly on their way to flying another. Musicians who have learned one instrument can learn a second or third with much greater facility than those who are just starting their first. Students, therefore, who study Latin and/or Greek will find they are on their way to learning additional languages (especially Romance languages) with much less effort.

Integration of Learning

I have mentioned that classical educators do not see subjects as self-contained and isolated. Knowledge is more like a web than a chest of drawers; there are no subjects that are unrelated to others. Literature, history, and theology, for example, are quite intertwined. Anything from the past (in any subject) can be history; anything committed to creative or excellent writing can be literature; and any subject considered in relation to God and biblical teaching can be theology. Until the nineteenth century, educators understood and taught knowledge as a web, rather than as separate departments. Classical educators, therefore, while teaching classes in "history" or "literature" keep the boundaries light and fluid and emphasize the inter-relationship of all knowledge.

The teaching of Latin is an apt example of how classical educators integrate knowledge. Latin really is not a simple, self-contained subject. Latin is found virtually everywhere. It is found in all English writing (since 50 percent of English words come from Latin), so many classical teachers are constantly showing students those Latin root words, thus expanding their understanding and vocabulary of English. Latin is found in science. I recall the day my daughter came home with a science worksheet describing "carnivorous," "herbivorous," and "omnivorous" animals and delightfully showed me that one word was from *caro, carnis* ("flesh, meat"), one from *herba, herbae* ("grass, plant"), and the last from *omnis, omne* ("all"). Before her teacher told her, she knew what kind of animals were "territorial," "arboreal," and "aquatic" (of the *land, trees,* and *water*). Latin is found in literature. Much of the best literature up to about 1950 (and some afterwards) frequently contains Latin allusions or quotations. It is certainly in history, since the Roman Empire dominated Europe for at least a thousand years. Latin inscriptions abound not only in Rome but also in Washington, DC, and in American historical documents. Latin is in logic. All the fallacies of informal logic have Latin names, like *argumentum ad hominen* (argument to the man—abusing the person rather than addressing his argument) and *argumentum ad baculum* (argument to the stick—appealing to force to persuade someone to adopt your argument). As in logic, Latin is also in rhetoric. All of the figures of speech have Latin (or Greek) names, such as *alliteration* and *assonance*; the five basic rules (canons) of rhetoric all have Latin names, as well as their subcategories. Perhaps you can imagine the integration opportunities for other subjects like history, Bible, theology, literature, and science. They are legion.

Joining the Great Conversation Via the Great Books

Classical educators have always emphasized the importance of mastering the masters. Believing that there are real standards of beauty, goodness, and truth, they dared to pronounce some books good and some poor; they even went so far (over time) as to conclude some books the very best. In the old sense of the word, they were *discriminating*. Books that have been declared as great books by a consensus of informed critics over long periods of time we dare to call *classics*.[9] These books can also be judged by their influence—they are great books because they contain great ideas that have given birth to a great and ongoing conversation about what is beautiful, good, and true, and 99 other great ideas if we take Mortimer Adler at his word (he posits 102 great ideas).[10]

In classical schools, we seek to read the great books, the classics. We know that there is some great contemporary literature being published and we do read a sampling of the best we can find and judge in our own culture. We lean heavily, however, to those books which have proven themselves by their beauty, profundity, and shaping influence. Reading the classics also has the advantage of challenging our modern perspective, as C.S. Lewis aptly points out:

> It is a good rule, after reading a new book, never to allow yourself a new one till you have read an old one in between. If that is too much for you, you should at least read one old one to every three new ones. Every age has its own outlook. It is specially good at seeing certain truths and specially liable to make certain mistakes. We all, therefore, need the books that will correct the characteristic mistakes of our period. And that means the old books.[11]

---

9. What makes a classic? The word *classic* is flexible and ambiguous. It derives from the Latin word *classis*, which originally meant a "fleet of ships." It came to refer to groups of people—*classes* of people. In English it preserves this meaning, as in a *class* of 1st graders. It also has a connotation that means of the highest order—something *classy* is very good or *first class*. The Latin word *classicus* referred to the highest class of Roman citizens. The word *classic* preserves this meaning of being the very best. Thus scholars like Mortimer Adler refer to classics as books of enduring value. Books that are called "great books" are usually synonymous with "classics." However, books that are classics are enduring works, meaning they are older works, proven by positive assessment over time. It is possible for a new book to be a great book, but only after wide, critical acclaim and influence. It will take time, however, for new great books to become classics, if indeed they pass the test. Charles Van Doren referred to great books as "the books that never have to be written again."

10. In two volumes which preface the Great Books of the Western World series, Adler and William Gorman dedicate 10-page articles to each of the 102 "great ideas" which they find contained and discussed in the classic books of Western civilization. The two volumes are entitled *The Great Ideas: A Syntopicon* (Chicago: Encyclopedia Britannica, 1952; 31st printing, 1989).

11. C.S. Lewis, "On the Reading of Old Books," in *God in the Dock: Essays on Theology and Ethics* (Grand Rapids, MI: Eerdmanns, 1970), 202.

Starting in the grammar school grades, we choose children's literary classics from various times and genres. Examples include Aesop's Fables, fairy tales, and titles such as *The Courage of Sarah Noble, Peter Rabbit, The Boxcar Children, Little Women, The Door in the Wall, The Wind in the Willows, Johnny Tremain, King Arthur, Robin Hood, The Lion, The Witch and The Wardrobe, The Hobbit, Where the Red Fern Grows, Treasure Island, The Adventures of Tom Sawyer,* and *The Bronze Bow,* to name just a few. As students rise into the dialectic school, they begin to read books suitable to their development and burgeoning reasoning ability.

The Tools for a Life of Learning

We have all heard the proverb: give a man a fish and he eats a meal; teach him how to fish and he eats for a lifetime. By now I trust the reader can guess the application to classical education. We teach students how to fish, only they are fishing for knowledge and feeding their minds. The pole, the line, and the hook are grammar, logic, and rhetoric, always with them in their tackle box as they seek out wisdom, and eventually teach others.

Put another way, classical educators seek to teach students how to learn for themselves. If, for example, we compare logic to a sharp knife, we seek to impart to our students a very sharp knife indeed. There will always be wood enough to carve (other subjects and fields of knowledge); if we can give students a sharp blade, they can carve whatever new wood they find. This insight inspired Dorothy Sayers to refer to the trivium subjects as "tools of learning": a metaphor that has become prevalent among classical educators. Students who have mastered language—that is, who have mastered grammar and vocabulary, logical reasoning, and persuasive, eloquent speaking and writing—have the requisite tools necessary to study and master any subject they choose. We might hope they will be ready for college and the rest of their life.

We can imagine such a student in college tackling a new subject. He has learned in the early grammar years to approach a subject by breaking it down to its fundamental parts and mastering them by memorizing them—using chants, songs, and other mnemonic devices. He has learned during the logic years to study the ordered relationship among these parts, and to derive the principles that govern them. Finally, he has learned during his rhetoric years to discover how to take his acquired knowledge and communicate it effectively and creatively, applying it to new and varied situations and needs. Now he faces, say, anatomy for the first time. He would know how to start: (1) break it down to the fundamentals (various parts of the human anatomy) and master these, using songs, chants, and such; (2) study the relationships of these fundamentals (e.g., the relationship between the skeletal and muscular systems); and (3) write and speak clearly on what has been learned, applying and integrating this knowledge in new settings. Anatomical vocabulary, strange to his peers, would be friendly to him, all based in Latin and Greek which he has studied.

I have used anatomy as an example of how a classical education should prepare students for lifelong study. Some think that a classical education may prepare students for further studies in English, language, or history, but not scientific subjects. Historically, this has not been the case. The trivium arts lead to the quadrivium arts; the mastery of language leads to the mastery of science. The great scientists of the past were virtually all educated classically. Mortimer Adler cites the education of the great German scientists of the last century:

> The connection of liberal education with scientific creativity is not mere speculation. It is a matter of historical fact that the great German scientists of the nineteenth century had a solid background in the liberal arts. They all went through a liberal education which embraced Greek, Latin, logic, philosophy, and history, in addition to mathematics, physics, and other sciences. Actually this has been the educational preparation of European

scientists down to the present time. Einstein, Bohr, Fermi, and other great modern scientists were developed not by technical schooling, but by liberal education.[12]

Douglas Wilson cites another famous German scientist and chemistry professor, Bauer, who, when asked if he preferred new college students who had been "scientifically" or classically educated, answered that he preferred the later. Bauer said that after three months in college the classically educated students surpassed the others who had taken more science courses. He believed that classical students had the best-trained minds, which uniquely prepared them for science study. "Give me a student who has been taught his Latin grammar," he said, "and I will answer for his chemistry."[13]

Whether science or literature, history or philosophy, law or medicine; whether business or art, politics or ministry—the classically educated student will be prepared for study, mastery, and achievement. He should fish well.

Classical education, then, is a lifelong process of applying the "tools of learning"—tools that are the skills entailed in grammar, logic, and rhetoric and that travel with the student through his various stages of learning. The tools are sometimes called grammar, logic, or rhetoric, as are the stages (called by Sayers the poll-parrot, pert, and poetic stages). The following diagram portrays a "wheel of education" that integrates both the tools and stages of classical education.

---

12. Mortimer Adler, *Great Ideas from the Great Books* (New York: Washington Square Press, 1961), 106.
13. Wilson cites this conversation between Francis Kelsey and Bauer in his book *Recovering the Lost Tools of Learning* (Wheaton: Crossway, 1991), 89.

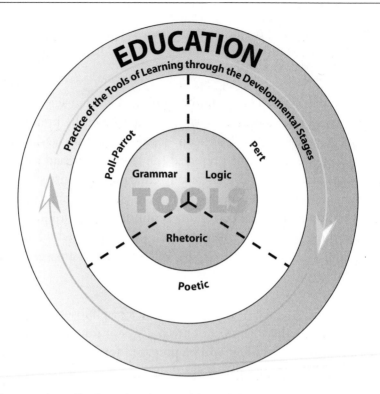

EDUCATION

Practice of the Tools of Learning through the Developmental Stages

Poll-Parrot

Pert

Grammar | Logic

TOOLS

Rhetoric

Poetic

Students are classically educated as they travel forward through the three stages of grammar, logic, and rhetoric, and so acquire the tools of learning that each stage imparts.

Peace, Rigor, and Delight

G.K. Chesterton pointed out that teaching a child involves disruption and a kind of educational "violence." Students are compelled to lay aside their notions of free play and come to a building where a score of adults insist they work hard at subjects we thrust upon them. Chesterton writes, "Education is violent; because it is creative. It is creative because it is human. It is as reckless as playing on the fiddle; as dogmatic as drawing a picture; as brutal as building a house. In short, it is what all human action is; it is an interference with life and growth."[14] This is to say, classical educators acknowledge that education is hard work—for

---

14. Chesterton, *What's Wrong With the World*, 166.

teacher and pupil. I say this after declaring earlier that students generally delight in a classical education, that we teach them the way they want to be taught. I still hold this as true. But I also believe that hard work and academic rigor do not exclude delight. Classical educators hold to the paradox that joy and labor can live together. Yes, something is being given up (play, TV, video games, etc.), but something wonderful is being gained (another language, new and thrilling books, the marvels of history, science, and math). Neil Postman has helped us see how TV has left us with the notion that all education must be entertaining or amusing.[15] This way of thinking is persuasive, but erroneous. Children can find even deeper pleasures than the TV and find them through rigorous work toward high prizes.

Surely you remember working hard for something you prized—perhaps even your beloved. The words *student* and *diligence* retain this same ethos. *Studere* means "to be eager for" or "zealous." *Diligere* means "to love" or "to delight in." One can quickly see the connection: we are diligent about those things we love, whether people, knowledge, or skill. The diligent athlete loves to perform well, to win. The diligent lover stops at nothing to win his lady. The diligent musician practices for hours out of love for music and thirst for virtuosity, and the diligent student is captured by and zealous for knowledge, skill, and wisdom.[16]

So classical educators encourage students to live up to their name. We try to foster zeal, eagerness, and diligence; we try to hold

15. Postman's book *Amusing Ourselves to Death: Public Discourse in the Age of Show Business* (New York: Penguin, 1984) is a sustained exposition of the way TV has influenced and shaped the way we now communicate and think. He devotes one chapter to the ways in which TV has shaped education, arguing that "television's principal contribution to educational philosophy is the idea that teaching and entertainment are inseparable." Postman, 147.
16. James Sire has highlighted the importance of these "intellectual virtues" in his book *Habits of the Mind: Intellectual Life as a Christian Calling* (Downers Grove, IL: InterVarsity Press, 2000). This book is valuable reading for classical educators.

before them the beauty and allure of language, history, and math; we make an appeal to their hearts as well as their minds and model for them a passion for learning and study. We can do this best in a peaceful environment, with clear rules of student behavior. It may seem odd, but our children are generally happy and enthused (and they run and yell on the playground!) but are peaceful and secure. Enthusiasm and peace can also coexist.

Demonstrated Results

Any parent wants to know how classically educated students actually fare on standardized tests, in college, and in the workplace. They do so well that we must be careful how we view them and ourselves—for we are tempted to arrogance. In our belief, they do well not because we or they are so clever and smart. They do well because the proven methods of classical education enable them to. Students around the nation in classical schools typically score in the top 10–15 percent on national tests like the Stanford Achievement Test and Scholastic Aptitude Test (both abbreviated SAT). Established classical schools often graduate a significant proportion of National Merit Scholars (determined by PSAT scores) and students with extremely competitive SAT scores (in the top 5 percent).[17] Classically educated seniors have no trouble getting into good colleges, and many qualify for highly selective colleges and universities; a good number receive merit scholarships or other scholarships. Colleges around the nation have shown an interest in these students and have familiarized themselves with the classical approach and curriculum being recovered in the United States. Currently, classically educated graduates are attending such colleges as Johns Hopkins University, Grove City College,

---

17. Gene Veith and Andrew Kern have documented these results in their book *Classical Education: Towards the Revival of American Schooling* (Washington, DC: Capital Research Center, 1997), 24. The Association of Classical and Christian Schools (ACCS) publishes a yearly directory that lists the standardized test results of most schools in the association, and which indicate that ACCS schools on average score in the top 15th percentile.

Hillsdale College, Wheaton College, William and Mary, and Wake Forest, as well as numerous state universities such as the University of Virginia, Idaho, etc.

Classical schools are growing at a robust rate. It is not unusual for new classical schools to grow by 25–30 students per year until they reach a full K–12 program in 8–10 years with approximately 200 students. There are currently more than 290 schools in the Association of Classical and Christian Schools (ACCS), with new schools starting at a rate of about 10–20 per year. Classical homeschools are growing at an even faster rate, and there are more students receiving classical education at home than in traditional school settings.[18]

Partnership with Parents

Classical schools work with and for parents. Since we believe that it is the parent's responsibility (not the state's) to educate their children, it cannot be otherwise. Our authority over children is delegated to us from parents who have enlisted us to help them in their educational task. We see ourselves as *in loco parentis*—in the place of the parents. This does not mean that parents dictate the curriculum or pedagogy; it does mean that teachers serve the parents, listen carefully to their feedback about child and curricula, and seek to forge true relationships with parents in order to best understand and educate their children. It usually means that parents are welcome in the classroom; it means that parents take their responsibility seriously by reviewing and helping with homework, encouraging their child to be disciplined and diligent, and generally supporting the teachers and staff of the school.

---

18. While it is harder to measure the growth of homeschools, we do know that the majority of classical texts and materials are purchased by homeschoolers, indicating homeschooled students outnumber those in traditional schools.

When parents abdicate their responsibility to educate their children, it is inevitable that some other institution will step in to take over. T.S. Eliot warned that as parents become passive, the schools would increasingly replace parental roles and responsibilities:

> Instead of congratulating ourselves on our progress, whenever the school assumes another responsibility hitherto left to parents, we might do better to admit that we have arrived at a stage of civilization at which the family is irresponsible, or incompetent, or helpless; at which parents cannot be expected to train their children properly; at which many parents cannot afford to feed them properly, and would not know how, even if they had the means; and that Education must step in and make the best of a bad job.[19]

Parents at classical schools do not assume that education is the school's responsibility. They understand that the school is assisting them to fulfill *their* responsibility. Many parents choose to classically educate their children at home; these parents are certainly taking their education responsibility to heart. However, most parents have themselves not been classically educated. We are, after all, recovering something that has been neglected for at least two generations. So parents are learning along with their children. Many a parent at classical schools is studying Latin along with his or her 3rd grader; many parents are finally learning English grammar, or studying logic. As you can imagine, this kind of collaboration and commitment among parents, teachers, and students involves a good bit of hard work. Parents in classical schools think this labor is worth the prize, not only for their children but for themselves. To varying degrees, we are all trying to get the education we were not given.

On any given night, parents are encouraging children as they do homework. They are checking homework, reading notes

19. T.S. Eliot, *Christianity and Culture* (Orlando: Harcourt Brace & Co., 1939), 181.

from teachers, writing or calling teachers, and helping students stay organized and ready for what lies ahead. Beyond this, they are reading to their children; praying with them; instructing them in a myriad of ways around the house and the dinner table; discussing books, field trips, and the experience of the day; and counseling and exhorting them regarding peer relationships, schoolwork, homework, chores, and play. They are parenting. The school helps them parent, but does not become the parent. Parents come onto campus and into classes as they wish; they assist in classes, substitute, come on field trips, help serve lunch, or coach a team. Many teachers are parents with their own children in the school; board members are parents; administrators are parents. Parenting and educating, in such a school, are not easily distinguished.

Christian and Classical Education

The school where I served as headmaster was started in order to recover classical education, but the most important aspect of the school is its Christian orientation. Classical education was inherited by the church, with some modifications, and put into service for centuries. We are continuing in a tradition, therefore, that is both classical and Christian. The ancient Christians saw that Jesus Christ must have preeminence in the academy as in all of life. In an age when so many Christians have facilely neglected the life of the mind and adopted the agenda and outlook from secular institutions, we are seeking to recover an outlook that honors Christ as Lord of every discipline, subject, and institution. We see both the academic and spiritual recovery as intertwined, and seek to repent for our neglect of both. We have not loved God with all of our hearts or minds.

Many Christians find it challenging to unify the two halves of their head that were once split into the sacred and secular, and to begin thinking "Christianly" about all areas of life. But it is being done. Our curriculum does not contain one lonely Bible course as a means of making our education Christian; it seeks rather to integrate Christian teaching in every subject, including . . . math. Even simple equations like 2 + 2 = 4 have a Christian dimension.[20]

Until a hundred years ago, Christians were in the forefront of all cultural institutions, shaping politics, business, philosophy, science, literature, music, and art. The reasons for the decline of Christian influence are complex and varied, but the abdication of Christians in the field of education is a major contribution. In 1961, Harry Blamires could write, "There is no longer a Christian mind." Since 1961, I am glad to say, there has been a good deal of ground regained, but nothing approaching what was once held.[21] Classical educators are seeking to help recover the Christian mind and prepare extraordinarily equipped leaders who "can take every thought captive for Christ" and shape and lead the cultural institutions of our society.

Shepherding Hearts/Intellectual Virtue

So you see that we are committed to the life of the mind. But as Christian educators we know that a student is not a disembodied mind, but a person with a soul and a heart. We can never teach a mind only, or a heart only; we are always teaching a person with both. Consequently, we cannot shirk our responsibility to address and cultivate the spiritual and moral dimensions of

---

20. Mathematician and theologian Vern Poythress has shown that "2 + 2 = 4" is neither religiously neutral or undisputed. He writes: "It may surprise the reader to learn that not *everyone* agrees that '2 + 2 = 4.' If with Parmenides one thinks all is one, if with Vedantic Hinduism he thinks that all plurality is illusion, '2 + 2 = 4' is an illusory statement. On the most ultimate level of being, 1 + 1 = 1. What does this imply? Even the simplest arithmetical truths can be sustained only in a world-view which acknowledges an ultimate metaphysical plurality in the world—whether Trinitarian, polytheistic, or chance-produced plurality." Vern Poythress, "A Biblical View of Mathematics," in *Foundations of Christian Scholarship* (Philadelphia: P & R, 1975), 86. For Poythress it is the Christian doctrine of the Trinity which preserves mathematical unity and plurality, thus sustaining the real unity and plurality in equations like "2 + 2 = 4." See also James Nickels, *Mathematics: Is God Silent*, which explores an explicitly Christian view of mathematics.
21. Thirty-three years later, in 1994, Mark Noll could write, "The scandal of the evangelical mind is that there is not much of an evangelical mind." Noll, *The Scandal of the Evangelical Mind* (Grand Rapids, MI: Eerdmans, 1994), 3. He quotes Blamires (*The Christian Mind: How Should a Christian Think?*) and makes his assessment of a very partial recovery, and urges Christians to complete the task.

our students. Ancient educators like Plato and Quintilian argued that students must be taught virtue, Quintilian going so far as to say that only the good man could be a good orator. Character has always been a chief goal of classical education. Christian educators have historically emphasized that education and study is a part of Christian discipleship—an expression of loving God with all our heart, mind, and strength. John Milton put it very well:

> The end of learning is to repair the ruins of our first parents by regaining to know God aright, and out of that knowledge to love him, to imitate him, to be like him, as we may the nearest by possessing our souls of true virtue, which being united to the heavenly grace of faith makes up the highest perfection.[22]

Christians should see that all knowledge is, in an ultimate sense, knowledge of God himself and an attempt to reverse the curse and head back to Eden where we can be closer to God and become more like him. That is, Christians face frankly the reality of sin in education and see all knowledge as a means of knowing God, and in so doing attaining "true virtue."

From this perspective, then, education entails ongoing repentance and spiritual war. Since the fall of Adam this has been the Christian task, and no less so in education. Students, therefore, need guidance, correction, training, and rebuke, just as they need encouragement, commendation, and praise. They need academic discipleship. To this end, classical Christian educators cannot simply teach subjects; they must teach students made in the image of God. As teachers, they are also shepherds.[23]

---

22. John Milton, "On Education," in *The Harvard Classics*, vol. 3 (New York: Collier and Sons, 1910), 286.
23. Ted Tripp has written a comprehensive treatment of child-rearing entitled *Shepherding a Child's Heart*, in which he argues for leading children to an inward and enduring change by appealing to their hearts and consciences through an application of the Christian gospel. This book has guided many classical educators as they form and implement discipline practices in schools and homeschools.

Some Objections

Now some who hear of classical education, and even some who experience it, will offer objections. To many it sounds old and stuffy, calling to mind images of crusty schoolmasters rapping resentful students across the knuckles. Our talk of order and peace is sometimes received as "strict, cold, and constrained." Some, with a nod and a wink, whisper words like "rote learning" and fancy they have put all of classical pedagogy in its proper place. Classical education, to these people, can only be imagined as dreary, rigid, repetitious, dry, antiquarian, and culturally out of step.

Because classical schools have raised the academic bar and expect children to accomplish far more than they typically have in the last fifty years, some charge us with harshness and an undue emphasis on academics. Because classical students typically perform in the top 15% of the nation on standardized tests, some charge elitism and suspect that only gifted students are suited for classical schools, or that these are the only students we really welcome. Then comes the related charge of arrogance and pride, for what else could compel us to announce that our students regularly outperform their peers in other schools?

Then there are objections to classical curricula generally. Latin in 3rd grade? Logic for three years, starting in 7th grade? To some who have never studied a single foreign language, or who can barely remember a phrase after three years of high school Spanish (most of us), the study of Latin in the 3rd grade seems preposterous. Why study a "dead" language that is not only irrelevant but difficult? And to many, logic is a college-level course that seems dry and obscure.

Finally, classical schools often don't offer as much in the way of athletic programs and extracurricular activities. This is due in part because they are usually young schools that are still developing, with time and money in short supply. It is also due to the priorities that govern classical schools, which rank academics above other programs. This chief commitment to academics is criticized by some as lopsided, unbalanced, and stuffy.

I will respond to each of these criticisms. It does not follow that an orderly, peaceful school must therefore be harsh and cold. It is possible to have respectful, disciplined, and diligent students in a warm, enthusiastic setting. It is possible to be serious about one's work without being serious about oneself; it is possible to be both industrious and joyful. We grant that it is rare, but we maintain that it is being recovered.

The charge of elitism cannot be established simply on the basis of strong student performance. Classical schools are typically a cross-section of the community with common ratios of average and gifted students. In my experience, the reason that classical students score well on standardized tests is because classical teaching methods really work and enable students to acquire skill and knowledge. In addition, classical students often acquire diligent and disciplined study habits, which can result in superior performance by students of normal intelligence. Whenever a student (or a school at large) excels academically, there is a temptation to pride. This is a weakness in classical education, and one for which we should repent whenever it appears. I would point out, however, that academic failure (or mediocrity) brings its own temptations—despair and apathy—which require their own repentance.

The objections to classical curricula are usually the result of our own ignorance—a form of xenophobia. We may criticize what is foreign to us. This is compounded since the curricula appear to be "old things" (like Latin) in an age that loves the endlessly new. Studying Latin seems like going backward to this mindset. It is clear, though, that something is not bad for being old any more than it is good for being new. It must be judged on other merits besides those of age, and the merits of Latin and logic study are numerous.

It is true that newly established classical schools do not have much to offer in the way of athletic and extracurricular programs. This is true of most new schools of any stripe. It is also true that classical schools emphasize academics, precisely because good academics are what American schools often lack. This is not to say that classical schools don't value athletics and other activities—they do. However, these come second to a strong academic program, as a new school's limited resources must go to academics first. In the early stages, schools often look to volunteer help in order to establish athletic and extracurricular programs.

Heading Home

If we dare call the classical education movement a movement, then it must be going somewhere. As I have said, we think we are moving backward and forward at the same time. We are going home in order to move out. And if we take the further audacious step and call what we are doing a revolution, then we had better be *re*-volving or turning back to our friends from the past who were educated so much better than we. We should be resolved to work hard; and we should expect opposition, for not everyone will understand and appreciate this endeavor. Popular culture is set against us; our own shabby educations are set against us. And we should be patient, for this task will take time. What was lost in a generation or two will likely take as long to fully recover.

We swim upstream, resolved not to be carried along with the current.[24] We have tasted something old, becoming new again; we have an inkling of a profoundly better mind and spirit, a continuing conversation with great minds, with each other, with God himself. Books, rather than the TV, have enchanted us once again:

---

24. Chesterton has also said somewhere, "Dead things flow with the current; only living things swim upstream."

From the heart of this dark, evacuated campus
I can hear the library humming in the night,
A choir of authors murmuring inside their books
Along the unlit, alphabetical shelves,
Giovanni Pontano next to Pope, Dumas next to his son,
Each one stitched into his own private coat,
Together forming a low, gigantic chord of language. . . .

I hear the voice of my mother reading to me
From a chair facing the bed, books about horses and dogs,
And inside her voice lie other distant sounds,
The horrors of a stable ablaze in the night,
A bark that is moving toward the brink of speech.[25]

Libraries fascinate and allure us. We hear these murmuring authors and grow irritated at being outside of the conversation; we force our way in, pulling Dumas and his son off the shelf, buzzing in our briefcase all the way home. We spend more money than we ought at bookstores and seek used books on the internet. Some of us, like Billy Collins (the poet quoted above), remember our mothers reading to us; most of us read books we should have been given to read long ago. We read to our children.

We think of our mothers, we read to our children; looking to the past we set our gaze as well to the future. Classical educators are hopeful and forward-looking; they seem to think the excellencies of the past are the best preparation for what lies ahead. They all concur that while times change, human nature does not, making books and the voice of our mothers reading to us some of the deepest things we know, and the most profound gifts we can pass on. Classical education turns out to be, at bottom, the love of our children to whom we give the best we have received.

I hope some of your questions have been answered; no doubt, many more have been raised. But I also hope there has been something like a ring of truth sounding through these pages, or

---

25. Billy Collins, *Sailing Around the Room* (New York: Random House, 2001), n.p.

perhaps a sense of corresponding parts fitting together, a puzzle being assembled. Of course there is more to learn; to this end, I have included a bibliography that can guide your queries. If your eyes have not seen what we say exists, visit a classical school, co-op, or homeschool and arrange to see the evidence—the children who embody the past and the future. We are confident they will spark additional interest and further . . . questions.

Bibliography

General Works Pertinent to Classical Education

G.K. Chesterton, *What's Wrong with the World*

T.S. Eliot, *Christianity and Culture*

C.S. Lewis, *God in the Dock*

Mark Noll, *The Scandal of the Evangelical Mind*

Thomas Oden, *After Modernity, Then What?*

Neil Postman, *Amusing Ourselves to Death: Public Discourse in the Age of Show Business*

E.K. Rand, *Founders of the Middle Ages*

James Sire, *Habits of the Mind: Intellectual Life as a Christian Calling*

Paul Tripp, *Age of Opportunity*

Ted Tripp, *Shepherding a Child's Heart*

Richard M. Weaver, *Ideas Have Consequences*

Works on Education

William Bennett, *The Educated Child*

E.D. Hirsch, Jr., *The Schools We Need & Why We Don't Have Them*

C.S. Lewis, *The Abolition of Man*

John Newman, *The Idea of a University*

Works on Classical Education

Mortimer Adler, *Reforming Education*

Augustine, *On Christian Doctrine*

Susan Wise Bauer, *The Well-Trained Mind*

Alan Bloom, *The Closing of the American Mind*

Stanley Bonner, *Education in Ancient Rome*

E.B. Castle, *Education Ancient and Today*

H.I. Marrou, *A History of Education in Antiquity*

John Milton, *Of Education*

Pierre Riche, *Education and Culture in the Barbarian West*

Dorothy Sayers, "The Tools of Learning"

Gene Edward Veith, Jr. and Andrew Kern, *Classical Education: Towards the Revival of American Schooling*

Douglas Wilson, *Recovering the Lost Tools of Learning*

Valuable Websites

The American Classical League: www.aclclassics.org

The Association of Classical and Christian Schools: www.accsedu.org

Classical Christian Homeschooling: www.classicalhomeschooling.org

Classical Academic Press: www.classicalacademicpress.com

The National Committee for Latin and Greek: www.promotelatin.org

The Well-Trained Mind: www.welltrainedmind.com

SPEAKING *and* CONSULTING

Dr. Christopher Perrin

Christopher serves full-time as the publisher of Classical Academic Press, and also speaks as an advocate for the recovery of classical education. See his full biography on the back cover.

Consulting

Christopher consults with those starting or seeking to grow classical schools and co-ops. He served for ten years as the founding headmaster of a classical school. He is especially adept at guiding schools through the establishment of an effective K–12 program and consults with administrators, boards, and teachers on all aspects of developing a thriving classical school. Christopher also provides staff training on a variety of topics, such as:

- *Staff and leadership development*
- *Developing student/intellectual virtue*
- *How to mentor and train new teachers*
- *Lower-school planning and development*
- *Upper-school planning and development*
- *Classical philosophy of education*
- *Origin and purpose of classical education*
- *History of progressive education*
- *Problem-solving with frustrated parents*
- *Enhancing communication among teachers, parents, and students*
- *Building partnerships among teachers and parents*

- *Building and keeping staff camaraderie and unity*
- *Establishing a positive culture among lower- and upper-school faculty*
- *Integrating logic throughout the upper-school curriculum*
- *Integrating rhetoric throughout the upper-school curriculum*
- *Classical curriculum development*
- *K–12 classical pedagogy*
- *Importance and value of Latin*
- *Importance and value of logic*
- *Importance and value of rhetoric*
- *Informal logic for every teacher*
- *Board consulting*
- *Parent and graduation events*
- *Custom consulting needs*

For more information about Christopher's speaking and consulting services (full descriptions and fee structure), please inquire at Consulting@ClassicalSubjects.com.

Speaking Engagements

Christopher speaks in a variety of settings, ranging from training events to keynotes. He is passionate about imparting the virtues of classical education to those contemplating the classical approach and about taking veteran classical educators to the next level. Christopher is an inspiring and informed veteran speaker. He frequently speaks on such topics as:

- *An Introduction to Effective Socratic Discussion: Why We Do It and How to Do It Well*

- *Loving the Things That Are Lovely: How to Cultivate Affection for the True, Good, and Beautiful in Our Students*

- *Learning from Rest: Cultivating Your Students' Habits and Virtues to Become Lifelong Learners*

- *The Tradition of Scholé: How Christians Pursued Restful Learning through the Ages and How to Recover It Today*

- *Why Children Must Play to Learn*

- *The Lighter Side of Education: How to Relax, Enjoy, and Laugh and Still Be an Educator*

- *Teaching Is . . . an Art*

- *Classical Education and the Common Core: The Latest Attempt to Make Technical, Bureaucratic Education Sound Good*

- Scholé *Homeschools: Why a School without Scholé (Leisure) Is No School at All*

- *Learning to Love What Must Be Done*

- *Classical Christian Education 101*

- *Revolutionary Latin: Why Latin Will Do Far More than Increase Your Vocabulary*

- *Revolutionary Logic: Why Logic Is Needed to Renew the Church and Culture*

- *How to Teach Latin in Grades 3–6*

- *Putting Together the Puzzle Pieces of Classical Education*

- *From Philosophy to Practice in Classical Education:* Multum Non Multa *(Much Not Many)*

- *The Monastic Tradition of Classical Education*

- *The Recovery of Memory—Before We Have Forgotten that We Have Forgotten*

- *The Liturgical Classroom: How to Make Your Class a Space for Tradition, Celebration, and Community*

- *A New (But Old) Paradigm for Describing Classical, Christian Education: Piety, Gymnastic, Music, the Arts, Philosophy, and Theology*

- *RetroACTIVE Education: Reaching Back to Go Forward*

- *G.K. Chesterton: The Man Who Laughed*

- *Embodied Learning: How to Help Students Love What Is Lovely*

- *A Concise History of Progressive Education: What Was Generally Wrong, but Occasionally Right, about Progressive Education*

- *Breaking Free of Your Own Modern Education and How Others Are Doing It*

- *How to Be a Teacher; How to Be a Student*

- *The Intellectual Virtues*

- *Logic 101*

- *Recovering the Classical Tradition of Education*

For more information about Christopher's speaking and consulting services (full descriptions and fee structure), please inquire at Consulting@ClassicalSubjects.com.

CLASSICALU
TEACHER TRAINING

We created ClassicalU with *you* in mind. We are confident this resource will inspire educators in schools, home-schools, and co-ops to dig deep into the richness of learning, no matter where you find yourself on your journey in classical education.

What You Get by Subscribing

New Content Regularly
Whether it's new courses, conversations, or interviews, we are always releasing new content to help you grow.

Ambrose Curriculum Guide
View more than 250 documents, including course guides for every class in a K–12 school or homeschool.

Downloadable Resources
Download notes, articles, recommended resources, and other files associated with our courses.

ClassicalU Community
Engage other educators and administrators in conversation and share ideas and resources.

Promotional Videos
Access professionally designed videos that promote classical education to grow your school or co-op.

Over 35 Self-Paced Courses!

COURSE LEVELS

1

Level 1: Apprentice
Begin your journey toward mastery.

2

Level 2: Journeyman
Continue your journey toward mastery.

3

Level 3: Master
Train to mentor and lead other teachers.

L

Level L: Lead
Grow as a lead or administrat

**Visit www.ClassicalU.com
to see free previews of every course.**